NADINE WILLIAMSON

The Peaceful Parent

How to Keep Your Cool and Raise Happy, Respectful Kids

First edition

ISBN: 979-8654866097

This book was professionally typeset on Reedsy.
Find out more at reedsy.com

Contents

Chapter 1: Why is Parenting Such a Struggle?   1

Chapter 2: What's Not Been Working for You and Why?   7

Chapter 3: Understand Why We Lose Our Cool   15

Chapter 4: The Path to A More Peaceful You   21

Chapter 5: How to Keep Your Cool- 4 Practical Pillars   25

Chapter 6: How to Deal with Your Kids While Keeping Your...   39

Chapter 7: What to do With Challenging Children   51

Chapter 8: The Power of Praise   69

Bibliography   73

Find Out More   77

Also by Nadine Williamson   79

Chapter 1: Why is Parenting Such a Struggle?

Let's face it; parenting can be tough. Much as we love them, our kids just have a way of pressing our buttons and pushing us to our limits. They make us see red, and we feel our stress levels boiling over. Suddenly, we find ourselves snapping or shouting in another futile attempt to gain control and perhaps some respect. Sound familiar? Well, don't worry, you're not alone. A survey of 2000 parents carried out by Bpme concluded that the average parent felt stressed with their kids at least six times a day.

So why is parenting so demanding?

This is such a complicated question to answer. Still, it's worth taking a little time to unravel what actually makes parenting so tricky. To be honest, some reasons are relatively timeless, and parents through the ages have had to deal with them. But some are very specific to our generation.

Don't be fooled... life is hard for everyone

In a technological world of social media feeds projecting endless images of supposedly perfect lives, it's easy to believe that you're the only parent struggling. But that simply isn't true. Don't kid yourself into thinking everyone else has it sorted and that you're the only one grappling to cope. You'll never see other people's stroppy kids, overflowing laundry baskets, or signs of depression when scrolling through Instagram. Believe me; you're not alone. We're all muddling through this stuff as we go along. No one's got it all figured out.

Sometimes life can be tough

Raising kids can be difficult for all of us, but for some, life just seems to throw in an extra curveball or two, just to push us to our limits. Maybe you're living in a volatile relationship, battling it out as a single parent, struggling for money or dealing with a physical or emotional disability. Perhaps you're caring for a parent, have lost someone dear to you or are tackling loneliness or isolation. Don't underestimate the impact that these things can have on you, your life and your ability to parent. Remember, none of us is superhuman. We're all just doing our best given the set of circumstances we find ourselves in.

Some kids are easier than others

Now, this isn't something we often like to admit, but it's true all the same. Have you ever noticed how some kids just seem to have a chilled and laid-back disposition? They happily sit and play, are rarely prone to tantrums and quickly drift off to sleep when tired.

We have to be honest and accept that some kids are more difficult to cope with than others. Some are highly strung, struggle with separation anxiety or insomnia. Others may face learning difficulties, illness or quite simply have a challenging personality.

We've all pitied the parent floundering with the purple-faced toddler, kicking and screaming in the supermarket. Maybe, like me, you've been that mum; sweating and anxiously trying to ignore the disapproving looks from passers-by, praying that the floor would swallow you up.

Let's just admit it; some kids are damn right tricky, and if this is the card you've been dealt, then you deserve a medal. But don't lose hope. I'll be teaching you a range of tools to help you keep your cool *and* manage even the most difficult of kids.

Recognise the influence of your own childhood

Like me, you probably hate blaming all of life's problems on your childhood, and it's important not to do so. But reflecting on your early experiences and understanding how these may affect your own parenting choices can be insightful and highly beneficial. Ideally, you will have been raised in a warm, caring home, where you felt completely loved, accepted and supported. If this was the case, then you'll now have a good template for how to raise your own kids. As a bonus, you'll probably also have the loving support of your parents and wider family, as you navigate your way through your own parenting maze.

But for many, this is not their reality. If your childhood was in any way abusive or neglectful, either emotionally or physically, then you may lack a positive parenting model to fall back on. Maybe you haven't figured out how your childhood experiences have affected you as an adult. If this is you, then you may find that seemingly trivial events trigger you, making you anxious, upset or angry but without understanding the reasons why. Trauma from childhood may have left you suffering from mental health issues such as anxiety, depression, low self-esteem, or addiction. Any of these could stop you from being the parent you want to be.

Even if your childhood was not traumatic, you might just have a desire to do things differently. But without a positive parenting blueprint, you may find this a daunting task. In challenging times, not knowing what to do can be confusing and stressful. You doubt yourself, which then makes effective parenting even more difficult.

We don't take care of ourselves

Despite our best intentions (and we all have plenty of those), most of us put ourselves at the bottom of our list of priorities. It's all too easy to get swamped by the demands of work, the school run, umpteen scheduled after-school activities and a mountain of housework. Not to mention the never-ending dilemma of what to cook for dinner.

We charge around in a constantly hyper-caffeinated, stressed out and sleep-deprived state. Multitasking, while forever focusing on the next job on our to-do list, becomes our everyday 'normal'. Yet we're so quick to berate ourselves for our 'bad parenting' when we don't measure up to our overly ambitious goals.

So just ease up on yourself a bit. When was the last time you got a full night's sleep or some real quality 'me time'? And I don't mean collapsing, exhausted, at the end of the day to scroll mindlessly through Facebook. Vegging out in a brain fog in front of Netflix doesn't count either... although we all love a box set binge sometimes.

I mean having a bubble bath, cooking yourself a healthy meal, going out for a drink with friends or simply taking time to sit on a bench in the park with a good book. Even if you have taken some time to look after yourself recently, was this a one-off or part of your routine?

Sleep every night for at least 7 hours if you can. I can't stress how important this is. So many parents struggle with pure exhaustion, making it harder to function in every way. Sleep deprivation makes us emotional, irrational and overly reactive. We can't think straight, maintain our attention or problem-solve effectively. Sleep is the cornerstone of good parenting, the metal in our armoury.

Remember your worth

It's so important to make yourself a priority too. How can you possibly expect to be everything to your family if you don't also take time to nurture and care for yourself? It doesn't work - they just end up with a worn-out version of you.

Chapter 2: What's Not Been Working for You and Why?

For many years, parenting has primarily fallen into two broad categories. Parents were either strict or permissive, and both camps had plenty to say about the failings of the other. Like me, you've probably tried to work out which of these suits you most. Unfortunately, children don't come with an instruction manual, and we can spend many years trying to work out the best way to parent.

We are heavily influenced by how we were raised ourselves. We either take the view that we want to be just like our own parents were or that we want to do it all completely differently. Perhaps we want to find a middle ground. Either way, at some point, most parents evaluate the merits of either strict or permissive parenting. The truth is that neither approach really works. Let's look at both to understand why.

The strict parent

Many parents, (perhaps those that consider themselves more 'old school'), hold the belief that being strict will make their children well behaved. In this approach, the solution to any problem is automatically determined by the parent. They present this to the child, usually in the form of an instruction. They lay down the law and expect the child to obey - end of story.

It is common for these types of people to have been raised by strict parents themselves. You might hear them say things like, "A smack never did me any harm!" This parenting approach is based on the belief that parents set rules and children should be punished when they disobey and rewarded when they comply.

In a way, I can understand the logic and sometimes these methods can be effective in the short term - well for a few minutes at least. After all, surely a child won't break the rules if they know they will be punished for doing so, right?

Unfortunately, it's not so simple. Strict parents believe that ruling over their kids in this way leads to them gaining their children's respect. But parenting through the use of fear and intimidation can never lead to genuinely respectful and happy children. They may behave out of fear of the consequences, but these kids often have troubled relationships with their parents, lacking closeness and respect. Beware, this is a high price to pay for obedience. Over time, these children do all they can to avoid their overly domineering parents. Once they disconnect in this way, parenting them can become increasingly challenging.

In life, we respect the people we trust; those who show us love and kindness. We may well treat those we fear 'respectfully', but this is not the same. When children genuinely respect their parents, they want them to be happy, and they hate to disappoint them. This makes raising them so much easier as the parent doesn't have to use fear to control them. But gaining this level of trust takes work and commitment. It's not the easy option, but it certainly pays off in the long run.

What kids learn from punishment

Punishment is a lesson in power, where the most powerful person wins. It doesn't teach kids to be reflective about their behaviour. Nor does it encourage them to want to be a better person. Instead, they mirror their parents and strive to dominate those around them.

Punishment teaches children to focus solely on how their behaviour affects themselves, with little regard for others. This does nothing to develop a child's sense of empathy. They may become selfish and do all they can to blame their actions on others to avoid being punished. Such children often learn to lie as a way of diverting blame away from themselves. Ultimately, kids raised in this way become preoccupied with avoiding punishment. They learn that if they do something wrong, even by mistake, they will probably be penalised and end up suffering in some way.

Punishment ends up with kids being less cooperative in the long term. Over time, the child views the parent as the cause of their suffering, and as such, they lose respect and begin to resent them. Eventually, many children stop caring about the consequences, as they become desensitised to them and start to rebel, resulting in less cooperation, not more.

The permissive parent

A permissive parent largely believes that the child should make the rules. Sometimes this is based on the assumption that the child knows what is best for themselves. However, permissive parents are often found to hate conflict and may use this approach to avoid a clash with their child.

This style of parenting typically leads to kids getting their own way. It's common for such children to develop a lack of empathy and self-control. Like overly disciplined children, they form a self-centred outlook, believing that the world revolves around them and that they are entitled to have whatever they want. These kids can find it difficult to consider the needs of others.

Both strict and permissive parenting result in one person winning while the other loses. Neither of these approaches are ultimately successful, as they fail to show kids how to take real ownership and responsibility for their actions. Neither do they teach children to understand the needs of others. In both approaches, kids ends up solely focused on themselves, but for very different reasons.

Luckily, there is a more balanced and productive approach: peaceful parenting. In this book, I'll be sharing this game-changing perspective and some brilliant strategies, to bring a sense of calm to your home and enhance the lives of your entire family.

Old habits die hard

We are emotional beings, but sometimes we try to suppress our feelings. Like it or not, it's natural to feel all sorts of things when faced with different situations. The only problem is that often it's not considered the 'done thing' to be emotional. For some people, this could be attributed to how they were raised. As children, they were taught not to cry, to have a stiff upper lip and to just get on with things.

Other people may feel that society puts them under pressure to keep their emotions in check; to handle every situation coolly and project an image of control. So many people do their very best not to let their feelings slip. Being seen to be emotional leaves them vulnerable and in fear of judgement.

But the fact remains, we all have emotions, and they come in many forms, be they good or bad. So, in moments of stress or pain, we may try to suppress how we feel, in the false belief that we can bypass our emotions and just deal with the situation. To help achieve this, we may attempt to distract ourselves by scrolling through our social media feeds or turning on the telly. Worse still, we may attempt to bury how we feel with food, alcohol or drugs, which poses obvious risks to our health. However, we usually find, to our detriment, that doing this merely results in our emotions inconveniently resurfacing at some later point, with more force than they had in the first place.

Others of us may struggle hugely to keep a handle on our feelings in stressful situations. Unable to bury them, we become overwhelmed and face an emotional crisis. We can lose ourselves in our thoughts, ravaged by our critical inner voice. In this state, we may experience fear, hopelessness or anger. Our behaviour might become erratic and we find ourselves crying, shouting or yelling. This only serves to push others away, leaving us feeling more isolated than before.

So, what are your habitual responses to stress?

It's worth taking a minute to consider what your habitual responses to stress are. By this, I mean, what is it you do almost without thinking, when faced with a stressful situation? Do you instinctively dive into the biscuit barrel and eat mindlessly to soothe yourself? Do you automatically start shouting at your family, nit-picking and micromanaging? Maybe you lose yourself in social media, take to online shopping, or reach for a bottle of wine?

It's essential to recognise that both blocking out emotions or becoming overwhelmed by them are two sides to the same equation; two opposite extremes. We need to work towards a middle ground, where we can become aware of our feelings, without overreacting. Then we need to take action to deal with the situation that triggered our emotions in the first place.

So, as a first step, try to recognise how you react to stress, as this awareness will help you to find a new path to a more balanced approach.

Next, it's crucial to allow yourself to feel what you feel. Rather than trying to resist your emotions or bury them, just identify them and acknowledge their existence. Remember that fighting against pain just makes us feel worse. We've all heard the saying, "What you resist, persists". Well, it's very true in this situation too.

Acknowledging how you are feeling doesn't mean you have to like the emotion, but it helps you to be honest about the reality of your current situation. You don't have to try and change your emotions either. It's important to remember that the only way out of our difficult emotions is to **go through** them. We have to allow ourselves to feel them first, before we can then process them in a healthy and balanced way.

Why yelling isn't the answer

When we get irritated, and our kids press our buttons, most of us tend to react by yelling. This is especially true if our own parents used raised voices to dominate or control us when we were little. Unfortunately, this hardly ever solves the problem, corrects our kids' behaviour or internal attitudes.

Think about how you feel when someone shouts at you. I'm sure you experience tension and anxiety in your body, along with an increased heart rate and shallow breathing as your emotions flare up and stress hormones seer through your body.

When we yell at our kids, they have the same response. The fear centre in their brain is stimulated, their instincts kick in, making them hyper-alert and self-protective. Their stress response causes them to either fight back, withdraw or run away. The last thing they can do in this state is listen to what you are attempting to communicate, never mind learn from it.

As adults, it's virtually impossible to maintain meaningful relationships with people who continually shout at us. Similarly, constantly yelling at our kids only serves to distance us from them. Over time, they grow to resent us and withdraw. A close relationship with them is the bedrock which allows us to parent them successfully. This is completely undermined when they become disconnected from us.

What's more, research has shown that being regularly exposed to yelling makes kids more aggressive, both physically and verbally in the long term. By continually shouting at them, we are modelling this for them; teaching them to shout to get what they want. We shouldn't be surprised if they then yell at us, their siblings, friends or other adults.

Yelling's not good for you either

Every time we shout, we set off our nervous system, and our stress hormones go sky high. If our default setting is to bawl at our kids, then we could be doing ourselves some long-term damage too. Living in a state of continuous stress can increase our blood pressure and weaken our immune system. It can also cause headaches, anxiety, depression and negatively affect our sleep patterns.

Regular yelling will, over time, quite literally rewire our brain. Each time we shout, the neuropathways our brain uses to do this become stronger and more established. Eventually, this can cause us to be more prone to raising our voice in other aspects of our life too.

I bet this isn't how you wanted it to be

As you bought this book, I suspect that you are probably in a position where your relationship with your kids hasn't quite turned out the way you had hoped. When we have children, none of us hope for a volatile relationship with them. When we hold that little bundle in our arms, we imagine a future filled with love, easy communication and close connection.

Take a moment to reflect on the last time you had a meltdown with your kids. Losing it is a horrible feeling, isn't it? I know - I've been there more times than I care to admit. It leaves such a sense of negativity between us and our children; a real disconnect. We wind up feeling guilty, isolated and just damn right sad. Every time we lose control, it knocks our confidence in our ability to parent. We feel disappointed and disillusioned. But don't lose hope. There is another way and I'll share some practical steps you can take to stop yourself losing control and help turn things around.

But before we go on, reflect upon your own parenting style. Are you strict or permissive or perhaps somewhere in the middle? Do you shout to control your kids or let them do as they please? How were you raised and how has this influenced you? By considering each of these, it can help you understand your own parenting makeup and how you came to settle on the methods you now use.

Think about what has worked well for you so far and what hasn't; which bits you want to keep and what needs to change. An honest evaluation of where you are at currently, will give you a great foundation upon which to build. Then you can consider each of the techniques I'm about to share with you. If they resonate with you, use them to develop a more peaceful style of parenting.

Chapter 3: Understand Why We Lose Our Cool

Before we can understand how to keep a cool head, we first need to work out what makes us blow up in the first place.

Physiology has a lot to do with it

Imagine the scene. It's 7.45am, you're late for work, and your 3-year-old is refusing to put their shoes on. They are lying on the hallway floor kicking and screaming, making it impossible for you to either get their feet into their shoes or manhandle them into the car. Here enters your stress response. You feel your heart racing, jaw tightening, and your anxiety levels soar as the frustrated rantings of your inner voice charge through your mind. The vital thing to remember here is that you are not choosing to react this way. At this moment, your stress response is acting on autopilot, and these reactions are happening all by themselves.

Let me explain. Our brains are made up of lots of different components, but to understand the effect of our stress response, we're just going to focus on two of them. Our prefrontal cortex (PFC) is situated right behind the forehead in the upper part of the brain. It controls decision making, logical thinking, problem-solving, creativity, and helps us to manage our emotions. Bear in mind that these are all highly valuable skills when trying to keep your cool when your toddler is kicking off.

It's also useful to know that most people don't have a fully formed PFC until they're in their early 20s, so your kids definitely don't have one.... that's right, they *don't have* the part of the brain that helps them to control their emotions. Explains a lot, don't you think?

The limbic system is located in the lower part of the brain and is mostly responsible for creating our big emotions and triggering our stress response. What's important to understand is that when our stress response is activated, our limbic system takes over and *bypasses* the PFC. The stress response actually *cuts off access* to the PFC, making it impossible for us to use the rational part of our brain in that moment.

So, becoming stressed out isn't a choice we make. It's the result of our biological systems reacting automatically. Is it any wonder, therefore, that our judgement and reactions often become impaired when dealing with challenging kids?

But is there another way? Instead of becoming highly reactive, what if we could respond calmly instead? Luckily, through intentional practise, we can train ourselves to react differently, and I will explain how to do this.

What happens in meltdown mode?

When we 'lose it', and by this, I mean 'lose control of our emotions and have a bit of a meltdown', we tend to feel a range of extreme feelings. These can include anything from anger, fear or sadness to guilt, shame and confusion.

We all have different personalities, and we all 'lose it' in different ways and with varying levels of intensity. Some of us scream, shout and slam doors. Others might go quiet, cry, get snappy, sarcastic or storm off in a huff.

We must reflect on and recognise our own particular style of 'meltdown' as this behaviour is the only thing we can control. That's right, we *can't* control what we *feel*, or our automatic reactions triggered by our stress response, but we *can* control our *behaviour* during a meltdown.

So remember, when you lose control, you are having an emotional reaction and not a rational one. There is very little you can do to control the emotions you are experiencing. Instead, *notice* how you *feel* so that you can *choose* how to *respond*. "Choose how to respond! How?" I hear you shout. Don't worry - we're getting to that.

Triggers: What are they and why do they make us lose it?

A 'trigger' is anything that makes us more reactive and puts us on edge. In a triggered state, people can quickly rattle our cage, causing us to 'lose it'. Of course, anyone can make us see red, but for the purposes of this book, we are just going to focus on kids, who as we all know, are expert cage rattlers.

In a calm situation, where everything is under control, we are unlikely to let our kids' antics bother us, and so they won't spark our stress response. Instead, we find ourselves able to patiently handle their behaviour, in a fashion that would make us proud.

Catch us in a triggered frame of mind, though, and it's a whole different scenario. Our nervous system throws us into a stress response mode. We see red, and suddenly any little thing our kids do rattles our cage. And they don't just stop at rattling. Now the little monkeys are jumping all over it, bashing those bars and making one hell of a racket!

Depending on how our day is going, we may be able to handle this for a while, but if we are anything near-human, eventually, we are seriously going to lose it. And sometimes that means real fireworks!

To manage our reactions, we need to understand what our triggers are and how to deal with them. By doing this, our stress response will be far less likely to be activated, and we'll be better able to stay calm.

Please take note of a fundamental fact here. You are going to learn how to make sure your cage is not so easily rattled, **not** how to stop your kids from bashing those bars altogether. This is because the only thing you can really control is **how _you_ respond**.

You need to accept that kids will always behave like kids. Expecting anything less from them is fanciful. Hanging your hopes of sanity on their ability to do anything else is asking for trouble. Having said that, we'll look at a range of strategies to help you manage your kids' behaviour too, but I just want you to be realistic.

Types of triggers

Some experiences, such as pain or exhaustion, will put anyone on edge, regardless of who they are or what their background is. Others are unique to individual people. For instance, I hate crowds, whereas you may feel comfortable in busy places.

Specific triggers may stem from a resent or short-term stress but have a clear end in sight. A broken arm or a challenging situation at work could be examples of these. Others, however, could result from long-term trauma and may affect our entire lives. These may be complicated to deal with and lead to us being more reactive than we otherwise may have been.

You might have control over some things that set you off, while having no sway over others. For example, I find the news upsetting, so I can turn it off. But I can't do much about the late-night partying at my neighbour's house every weekend.

Always remember that nothing stays the same. Things that upset you now may not matter further down the line. For instance, problems with your child' current class teacher won't be important next year. It's comforting to recognise the transient nature of these catalysts.

Being a parent can raise difficult issues, and you may find yourself facing things that you haven't encountered since you were young. If you were bullied at school and now have to deal with your own child being picked on, you may find this a traumatic experience which makes you highly reactive.

Take stock of your triggers

It's worth taking some time to take stock and focus on what really puts you on edge. Think back over recent occasions when you lost your cool with your kids and try to work out what sparked these situations. Perhaps you were exhausted and at your wit's end with money worries or concerns about work? Were you having difficulties with your marriage or maybe you were feeling lonely?

I know it's easy to think that the sole reason for you 'losing it' was your kids' poor behaviour. But dig a little deeper, and you'll probably discover the underlying trigger that made it possible for them to get under your skin in the first place. Be honest with yourself here. Understanding what sets you off and catalyses your stress response can be instrumental in helping to protect yourself against this in the future.

How to recognise that you've been triggered

So now that you understand what triggers are and have taken time to analyse what sets you off, it's crucial to realise when you have in fact been triggered. This is all about recognising the thoughts, feelings and behaviours that you display whenever this happens. Here are some common signs:

- Feeling like you have a short fuse and could lose your temper at any moment.

- Physical tension in your body. You might get tight shoulders or a headache.
- Anxiety and finding yourself dwelling on the same issue repeatedly.
- An urge to control and micromanage everyone around you.
- Struggling with a compulsive need to comfort eat, drink, or smoke to bury your emotions.

Chapter 4: The Path to A More Peaceful You

The good news is that you don't need to fix your triggers or even get rid of them. That's not the name of the game. Instead, focus on becoming *aware* of them. Next, you have to learn to *accept* them and finally you need to take some positive steps to *deal* with them. So let's consider some practical ways of achieving this.

Becoming trigger aware

The steps outlined in the previous chapter can help you recognise situations which might set off your stress response. Take note of your reactions when you notice yourself getting tense, and use them as early warning signals. For example, do you grit your teeth or hold your breath?

By keeping your awareness focused on your triggers and your reactions, you can catch yourself before you blow and take steps to calm the situation down.

Accept the presence of the trigger

When you've been triggered or are at risk of this happening, it's essential to accept that this is the case. In a stressful situation, we often try to fool ourselves into thinking we can deal with it without acknowledging our feelings or reactions. But time and time again, we find that this approach rarely works. The more we try to just battle through, the more worked up we become.

I can't emphasise enough how important it is, to be honest with yourself about this. If you know that your parents commenting on how you raise your kids sends you into an overly defensive mood, accept this as truth. Don't kid yourself into believing that their comments don't affect you when you know damn well that they do. By accepting your triggers honestly, you are then in a strong position to take decisive action to deal with them and stop yourself from losing your cool.

Dump or deal with your triggers

So, you've analysed, understood and accepted your triggers. That was the easy bit! Now, what are you going to do about them? Ideally, we'd love to get rid of them all, wouldn't we? But unfortunately, real life doesn't work like that. Much as you might like to get your overly opinionated grandmother to stop commenting on your parenting style, the chances of that happening may be slim.

If there are things you can do to permanently remove triggers from your life without upsetting those that you care about, then go for it. If you can give up the job you hate, then do it. If it's possible to cut ties with the neighbourhood busy body who brings you down every time you talk to her, then go for it! If a move to online food shopping is possible, so you don't have to drag your toddler round the supermarket, that's brilliant.

But for those triggers that you can't make magically disappear (and I'm afraid that means most of them), you have to learn to deal with them. In the next chapter, I'll give you some practical ways of doing this. But there are three things I'd like you to take on board before we get started:

1: Action is the key

I'm going to be a bit candid with you here. It's all too easy to read umpteen parenting books, digest the information on offer and then do nothing about applying your newfound knowledge. But for things to change you need to take action - do what you learn, don't just read about it. This takes commitment and perseverance in times of stress, when you're knackered, overstretched and just feel like throwing in the towel. But if you can push on through and make some real practical changes, you'll reap the benefits, both for yourself and your family.

2: Practice makes perfect

Like learning anything new, the more you practise, the better you'll get. And the same is true of this. The more you apply the techniques I'm about to teach you, the better you'll become at keeping your cool when all around you are intent on pushing your buttons.

3: When you stumble... and you will stumble

Accept right now that you won't always get it right. There will be days when, despite your best intentions, you'll get well and truly triggered. The kids will climb under your skin, boots and all, and you'll lose your rag most spectacularly! This is bound to happen because you're human and we all fall off the wagon sometimes, no matter what it is we are working so damn hard to achieve. And you know what - it's not ideal, but it's ok.

What's more important is what you do next. Do you throw your hands up, declare it's all a waste of time and simply resort to your old ways? No, absolutely not! In times such as these, pick yourself up and dust yourself down. Take some time to reflect on what went wrong and why, learn from your mistakes, forgive yourself and try again.

Chapter 5: How to Keep Your Cool- 4 Practical Pillars

F our core pillars stand at the centre of your ability to keep a cool head in challenging situations. Work on developing each of these as they hold the key to you successfully becoming a peaceful parent.

Pillar 1: Sleep: The cornerstone of it all

Getting enough sleep completely changes our perspective. It impacts on all the emotional, physical and phycological aspects of life. Sleep deprivation is serious business. Nothing makes us feel worse. It clouds our thinking, impairs our judgement and mood, and makes us far more likely to be triggered. So, if you are struggling with exhaustion, then you need to take some serious steps to address the problem.

How much sleep are you getting?

To start with, actively track how much you sleep. You might be surprised by the results. Often, we think we are getting more sleep than we are. Now, you can be all technical about this and use an array of gadgets and apps to do your sleep tracking, or you can just use a notebook to record the times you turn out the light and wake up. This may not be super accurate, but you'll get a good idea of how much you are sleeping and flag up any distinct patterns and potential problems.

Establish a sleep routine

Try to go to sleep and wake up at the same time every day, even at the weekends if you can. This helps your body and mind to get into a sleeping rhythm, which should make it easier for you to fall asleep and ensure you get enough rest.

Have a wind-down routine

I was always prone to keeping busy until the last minute of the day, and then collapsing exhausted into bed. I wondered why I couldn't sleep! I learnt that it's so important to give my body a chance to wind down. So now I try to take an hour before bed to relax and maybe have a bath or read a book. Just give yourself a bit of time to change gear and unwind, and you'll find it much easier to fall and stay asleep.

You need the dark to be able to sleep

Avoid screens at night if you can. I know we've all heard this before and the reality of not scrolling through our phones in bed or not watching TV last thing at night is hard to handle. But if you are genuinely struggling with sleep exhaustion and are frequently losing your cool with your kids, then isn't this a sacrifice worth making?

Any exposure to blue light from screens or any other type of bright light at night messes with your body's circadian rhythm, which can seriously hinder your ability to go to sleep. If you really can't manage without a screen before bed, then dim it as much as you can to limit its effect.

Be careful with caffeine

If you find yourself struggling to get to sleep, then try limiting your caffeine intake after 2 pm. While you're at it, don't be fooled into thinking that alcohol will help you sleep. It's a stimulant, so it is likely to hinder your hopes for a good night's kip. In fact, it's advisable not to have too much to drink of any kind just before bed to avoid those late-night toilet breaks.

Pillar 2: The right support

Let's be clear. No parent on this planet can properly raise healthy, happy kids without support. We're social beings and have evolved to depend on the help and input of others. Even with a strong support network, parenting can be bloody challenging at the best of times. Please don't underestimate the importance of having people to help you if you plan to come out of this thing in one piece.

All parents need help. Our nervous systems automatically calm down when we are in the presence of other adults who we trust and who make us feel safe. Spending time with other supportive people helps to keep our thoughts in perspective. We can acknowledge our successes and discuss our difficulties, tapping into the knowledge and experience of others for guidance. Good friends can help to build our confidence. They encourage us to have faith in our parenting ability, thereby decreasing the chances of us losing our cool.

Be careful who you lean on

Although it's vital that we all get support, it's also critical to make sure that we lean on the right people. For medical help and advice, it's always best to go to a medical professional such as your midwife, health visitor or GP. Other parents can be a huge source of information and support and being part of a parenting network can work wonders to stop us feeling isolated.

Sometimes families can provide the best support of all. But unfortunately, that's not the case for everyone. Some families are incredible, but some are anything but. Often families are ok, but just not available when we need them for a range of reasons. Maybe this is because of death, addiction or other forms of family disfunction. Or perhaps you just don't see eye-to-eye; they don't understand or support your parenting choices, or maybe you don't even feel like you can leave your kids with them.

Be warned; problems with families can involve severe triggers. If this rings true for you, then please know that it's ok to be sad about it. You may need to take some time to process this, as parenting without the support of your family is a big deal. However, you need to accept the situation and build on the positive relationships in your life instead.

Be careful about trying to change your family dynamics. Although dealing with family conflicts can sometimes be positive, it also has the potential to fail. Old patterns are hard to break. So, if you decide to attempt this, be sure to protect your head and heart. The last thing you want is to cause old triggers to flare up and make it harder for you to function as a mentally healthy and balanced parent.

Who do you need?

Be picky about who you choose to let into your life. Remember, the people who appear the most popular with a polished online presence may not be the best fit for you. When it comes down to it, you don't need popular. You need someone who understands you, who shares your values and outlook, and who will be there when the going gets tough. So, take time to work out who you are, what's important to you and what you have to offer. This makes it much easier to work out the kind of people you are looking for.

Remember that you are not going to 'click' with everyone you meet and that's ok. We all know people we don't gel with, and that's just part of being human.

Often, it's crystal clear why we don't connect with them, and sometimes it's not. The key is to accept it and be prepared to move on. You don't have to include everyone in your life. Be kind and gentle about it, but remember you're allowed to say no.

Ask, or you won't get

Ever felt lonely or isolated? I know I certainly have. But then I came to realise that everyone else was as caught up in their own stuff as much as I was in mine. They weren't mind readers. How were they to know that I needed a friend or some support if I didn't let them know?

I accept that it can seem like a big step to reach out in times of need, especially to people you perhaps don't know very well. But what's the worst that can happen? Maybe they'll reject you. But then again, they probably won't, and you'll develop just the kind of friendship you need. One thing's for sure; you won't know until you try.

Put in the effort

Remember that friendship is a two-way thing. In as much as you may need support, remember to show up for them too. In our busy lives, it can be all too easy to get caught up in the demands of the day-to-day but remember to take time to nurture your friendships. Rather than always waiting for an invitation or only responding to messages, try instigating them too. This will make your friends feel valued by you and help to maintain balanced and healthy friendships.

Pillar 3: Manage your tasks

Ever been in that situation where your kid pulls you up for saying 'hmm' repeatedly while they're trying to talk to you? But you're too busy focused on reading a post that just flashed up on your phone? You're aware that they're there and talking, but have no idea what they're actually saying… and they know it! They end up frustrated and angry with you because you don't give them your full attention. You then try desperately to redeem yourself while feeling decidedly guilty for your lack of quality parenting in that moment.

Or ever tried to check your kid's homework while on the phone? You quickly realise that you're not sure what the person on the other end of the phone just said, so you do your best to say something vague to hide your lack of attention. Meanwhile, you realise that you just can't focus on the worksheet in front of you either and so have to start over once you hang up.

It's time for the hard truth; sometimes multitasking simply doesn't work. Instead of making our lives easier, it just raises our stress levels and leaves us in a worse mess than we were before.

Appropriate multitasking - choose your tasks wisely

There are of course times when multitasking works just fine. There is nothing wrong with listening to a podcast while pairing socks; watching TV while cooking dinner or chatting on the phone while walking the dog. But if one of your chosen tasks could go wrong because it doesn't have your full attention, then abandon the idea of doing them together. If you are tired or stressed, it may also not be a good time to attempt multitasking. Similarly, if you are actively doing something with your kids, it may be best to focus on that alone.

Switch tasks, don't multitask

Instead, aim to be intentional and deliberate about switching between tasks. Rather than trying to do multiple things together, decide how to use your time efficiently to get jobs done one at a time.

For instance, spend ten minutes going through your child's homework with them so they understand what they need to do. Then leave them to work independently so you can prepare dinner. Agree to spend ten minutes together checking their work after the washing up has been done. In this way, everything gets the required amount of attention from you and is completed efficiently. However, you don't become overwhelmed by it all and resort to ineffective multitasking.

If it helps, write it down

If you're anything like me, you might find yourself jumping around between all the different jobs you need to do without completing any of them properly. I've discovered unwashed laundry in the machine at lunchtime, despite having loaded it at 7am. Distracted by my daughter's need for breakfast, I completely forgot to add detergent or press start on the machine.

Instead, I busied myself with making toast and preparing her packed lunch while sticking my cold coffee in the microwave to reheat for the 2nd time that morning. When I then went to heat my soup for lunch, I found my long forgotten (and now very cold coffee) in the microwave once again, not to mention the unwashed clothes in the machine!

This was not an uncommon scenario for me. I'll admit I have a brain like a sieve. But I found the solution was to write things down. This helped me to focus on what I needed to do and organise my tasks efficiently. By crossing them off once completed, my stress levels stayed much lower than before. Admittedly, I didn't have to add reheating coffee to my list, but you get the idea.

So, if are also prone to flitting around between unfinished tasks and not using your time efficiently, try writing them down and crossing them off your list once done. Similarly, if random thoughts keep popping into your head and you find yourself distracted by them; worried you might forget something, just write them down. This will help your mind to settle and focus on the job in hand.

Pillar 4: Learn to be kind to yourself

I know, I know, now we're getting into the territory of self-love and daily affirmations but bear with me. Take a minute to think about this. Why should you put all your energy and effort into trying to be the best version of yourself solely for the benefit of everyone around you? It's only right that you appreciate yourself too. You need to acknowledge that parenting is one of the biggest challenges that life throws at us, and you are doing your best. You may not always get it right; none of us do. But you are trying. (Otherwise, you wouldn't be reading this book!).

Allow yourself a bit of 'me time'

When you've been rushing around all day, looking after everyone else's needs, don't feel guilty for taking a bit of 'me time' too. If you can, ask your partner or a friend to watch the kids for a while. Go to a movie or spend an afternoon curled up on the sofa nattering to your bestie.

I know how easy it is to put your own needs at the bottom of the heap, but it's not right for you or your family. Also, ask yourself what that's teaching your kids? Remember that they'll model what they see. Do you want them growing up undervaluing themselves and never looking after their own needs? No, of course, you don't.

Besides, after a bit of a break, it's so much easier to get back onto the parenting wagon feeling refreshed and re-energised, which can only be a good thing for all concerned.

Watch how you talk to yourself

Have you ever noticed how you can be your own worst critic? Sometimes, without even realising it, we can be so harsh and unforgiving in the way we talk to ourselves. We rip ourselves to shreds with endless criticism and self-abuse. But why? We're all only doing the best we can. Would we treat anyone else so harshly? No, we wouldn't. So, handle yourself with some compassion, and realise that you don't deserve to be treated that way either.

Try to notice when you start berating yourself in this way and when you do catch yourself doing it, try instead to talk to yourself the way you would to a close friend. When you are kinder to yourself, your stress levels reduce. You'll then be far less likely to be triggered than if you're in a constant state of self-criticism.

Loneliness - the big deceiver

In our darkest moments, it's easy to feel isolated and to believe that we are the only ones going through this. But that's a lie you tell yourself; it's simply not true.

In moments such as these, do the opposite to what you feel like doing. Reach out to someone. This works better than anything else at dispelling the myth that you are alone. If you don't believe me, have a look at all the Facebook groups for lonely people. Try joining one - you may find the friendship and support you need.

Better still, phone a friend or a relative and arrange to meet up for a coffee. Get some real face-to-face human interaction into your life and you'll feel so much happier.

But above all else, don't listen to the lies you tell yourself. Remember, you're not the only one going through this. You're not alone.

Keeping your cool: Other tools in your kit

Besides the four pillars discussed above, there are a few other tools which you could carry in your emotional toolbox, to help you keep your cool. Let me go through them for you:

Declutter your life and mind

Sometimes too much of anything can be a bad thing. Maybe you're like me and find clutter to be a significant trigger. Too much stuff, information or choices and I feel swamped and overwhelmed. I operate better when my environment is tidy, when my schedule is less busy, and I'm not in information overload.

Take a look around. Are you feeling overburdened by too much of anything? Maybe a good clear out would help. I often find that my kids are the worst culprits, with toys, books and clothes overflowing everywhere. But do they need it all? Regularly cutting back and thereby limiting choices can lead to a calmer and happier life.

Are your kids' schedules jam-packed, leaving you run ragged and exhausted? If so, reassess and cut back. Kids need downtime too. You may well find that by simplifying their manic lives, your children will become more relaxed and contented. You'll feel under far less pressure too.

Are you in information overload, constantly scrolling through the news apps for the latest updates? If so, simplify. Choose one and check in twice a day. The world won't end if you're not up to date with the latest developments at every moment. You'll catch up soon enough. But your mind will be calmer, and you will be less stressed and reactive as a result.

Put your phone down - if you reach for your phone every five minutes, learn to leave it be for a while. Recognise that your brain needs time to chill out.

Take active steps to not continually bombard yourself with information. Be mindful and selective about what and who you expose yourself to.

Want to destress? Then move

I'm sure you've heard this before, but exercise reduces stress. When you're triggered, your body releases stress hormones. Exercise reduces these, relieving tension and helping you to keep a cool head. It also raises your serotonin level, (often called the happy hormone), leaving you feeling more relaxed and optimistic; helping to protect your mental well-being.

If you've had a stressful day, exercise gives you an outlet for all that pent-up energy and frustration. By choosing to exercise, which often means removing yourself physically from a stressful environment, you give yourself some much needed time out. This can be incredibly helpful in allowing you to take stock and reflect away from many of the triggers of your day-to-day life.

But it's critically important that you do something you enjoy. If you hate team sports, there's no point in forcing yourself to join the local netball team. If the gym is your idea of hell, but you love fitness classes, then sign up for aerobics or Pilates. If swimming or going for a brisk walk is more your thing, then choose those.

If the idea of exercising fills you with dread, then you have chosen the wrong activity. Decide what works for you, but just make sure you move, get your heart rate up, and you'll find that your mood and mental health will benefit tremendously. Try to do this for an hour, at least three times a week, to get the most out of it.

Find a moment of quiet

Noise surrounds us. TVs, endless devices, screaming kids, noisy neighbours, traffic: it's everywhere. It's one of my primary triggers, and it may be for you too. We all need silence, even if it's just for a few minutes each day. A little quiet time dramatically helps to reduce our stress levels, giving us a chance to breathe and regroup.

Try to take active steps to engineer yourself a moment of silence each day. Deliberately turn off the radio or TV and put your phone on silent. If you need to leave the house for a while to achieve this, then do so. Go and sit on a park bench for a few minutes if necessary. Just find a way to give yourself that little bit of time out.

Learn a different way to breathe

When stressed, your body tenses up and your breathing becomes shallow. Sometimes you can even hold your breath without realising it. This all adds to the tension in your body. Try deliberately taking slow deep breaths to dramatically help reduce your stress levels. This increases oxygen to your brain and slows down your heart rate.

Don't worry about how many breaths to take or how long to hold each one for. But when you find yourself in potentially triggering situations, stop for a moment or two to breathe deeply before returning to face the storm. You'll find that this vastly improves your ability to keep a cool head.

So, we've focused on the four practical pillars needed to help you become less reactive in stressful situations. To recap, these are the need for sleep, a good support network, learning how to manage your tasks efficiently and look after yourself properly. We've also looked at additional tools to help you, namely avoiding clutter, getting some exercise, finding a quiet moment and learning to breathe deeply. Hopefully, these techniques will help you stay calm and work towards being a more peaceful parent.

But that's only half of the equation when it comes to creating a peaceful home. Yes, of course, it's essential to learn to recognise your own triggers and develop strategies to regulate your reactions effectively. But that implies that the buck stops there. As we all know, coming up with pragmatic strategies to manage the behaviour of our children can be equally challenging. So, what can we do about that? Fear not! In the next chapter, I'll discuss some practical techniques to help you handle the most taxing of little people.

Chapter 6: How to Deal with Your Kids While Keeping Your Cool

I really hope you haven't just skipped ahead to this chapter! Tempting as that may be, it's essential to do the groundwork within yourself first. You need to take the time to understand what triggers you and why. You should reflect on what your automatic responses are when stressed, and how they came to be your default setting in the first place. Finally, by implementing the range of strategies I have shared, you can learn how to keep calm when your kids do their best to press your buttons.

By developing a deeper understanding of yourself first, you'll be far better prepared to face the frequent challenges of everyday parenting. So, if you haven't already done so, I urge you to work through the previous chapters before moving onto this one.

With all that said, if you're ready to learn some practical tools to manage your children's difficult behaviour, let's make a start.

Expect strong emotions

Kids are little humans, and they, just like us, have a range of emotions, that can sometimes be irrational, volatile or unpredictable. Remember that, (as explained in Chapter 3), children **do not** yet have a fully developed prefrontal cortex (PFC); the part of the brain that helps them to regulate their emotions and behave rationally. So, it's only right and fair to be sympathetic and understanding when they 'lose it' sometimes.

Remind yourself that you have had all your years on this planet to work out how to manage your feelings, but they are just starting out. Prepare yourself by being realistic - expect your kids to have powerful emotions. That way, you won't get caught out. But that doesn't mean you have to put up with bad behaviour. Our mantra in this is: expect strong emotions but limit unacceptable behaviour.

Start with the most obvious

If your child is kicking off, make sure you cover the basics first. Are they hungry, thirsty, tired or sick? Maybe they just need to get out of the house for some fresh air and a run around? So often we look for complicated reasons when our kids misbehave, when seeing to their basic needs will quickly solve the problem. So, go through each of these first to make sure you have the obvious bases covered.

See things through their eyes

Your child's view of the world may differ greatly from yours. It's easy when we are so wrapped up in the business of our own day-to-day lives, to misunderstand our children's perspective. But if your kids are being difficult, it will be for a reason; you need to recognise that something is bothering them. Try to take some time to see the world through their eyes.

Your child's age and stage of development will significantly affect their view of the world. For instance, babies cry to get your attention and to ensure that they get their needs met. They have no other way of communicating what they need, so try to imagine yourself in their booties.

All toddlers are prone to tantrums. This may appear 'naughty' to you, but toddlers' brains are still developing at this age, and so they cannot properly control their emotions. As children move onto being school-aged, they strive for independence, often pushing boundaries which can make them trickier to handle. But this too is a natural process and a necessary part of growing up.

Older children and teenagers are swamped with hormonal changes. They may experience difficult emotions which can be both frightening and challenging for them. They are often moody and withdrawn, both of which are very normal for children of this age.

Do you know what's happening in your child's world?

Are you aware of who's in their friendship group or what their latest interests are? Is there something troubling them they haven't shared with you? Things that may seem insignificant to you may be causing your child considerable distress.

Are they having problems with friends? Perhaps they're concerned about their image, or struggling with schoolwork? Are there difficulties within the family? Maybe they're dealing with separated or arguing parents, a bereavement, or could it be that they're not getting along with a sibling?

Do they perhaps feel that you don't have time for them as you're always working? Maybe they've realised that you're worried about money and this has caused them to feel anxious too? Perhaps they're concerned about a sick pet, their imaginary friend or are scared that there's a monster under their bed.

Learning to use empathy in parenting is a critical tool. But try not to rush this; don't make assumptions as you might jump to the wrong conclusions. Understanding your child's view of the world takes time, lots of listening and thoughtful conversation. You can't do this without forging a connected and close relationship based on trust and empathy. But how do you achieve this? Here are some useful techniques:

Listen carefully

When your child wants to tell you something, stop what you're doing, and listen with your full attention. They'll know if you aren't listening properly; they're rarely fooled by this one.

Be reflective in your listening; show that you've heard what they've said and maybe ask a couple of genuinely interested and relevant questions. Be careful not to turn your conversation into an interrogation by bombarding them with questions. Tempting as it may be, avoid swamping your child with advice. The most important voice in this conversation is theirs.

If they confide in you, it's equally important to acknowledge their emotions. Don't play down their feelings or try to persuade them that 'it's not that bad'. Just allow them to express what they feel and be in that moment with them in an empathetic and loving way.

By giving your child your full attention, they'll feel valued and connected to you. Make listening in this way a habit, and in time they'll learn to trust and confide in you. If you only give them half your attention, while busily doing something else, they'll soon stop communicating with you. They'll realise that you're focused on other things and won't feel like they're your priority. Often kids kick-off just to try to get your attention. You can usually avoid this by giving them your focus and actively listening to them.

Label your child's emotions

Sometimes your child may open up to you, explaining an entire sequence of events which has upset them. While *you* may be able to understand the emotions they are feeling, *they* might not. If you can tell that your child is feeling nervous, then saying, "It's normal to feel nervous before a school play," could really help them.

Don't assume that they know what they are feeling. By helping your kids to identify and name their emotions, they feel understood and comforted. This enables them to develop a vocabulary for their feelings so they can express themselves without the need for tantrums or unwanted behaviour.

Model what you'd like to see

Our kids watch and learns from us, and they model their own behaviour based on what they see. It's therefore vital that you demonstrate the actions you want to see coming from them and not the ones you don't.

If you lose your temper quickly and snap at those around you, then there's a good chance your kids will do the same. If you're messy and unorganised, they'll no doubt learn this from you. If it's important to you that they adopt a healthy diet, then they need to see you making good food choices for yourself. If you want them to be kind and generous, then let them see you putting this into practise in your own life.

Set healthy boundaries

When our kids see us taking care of our own needs, they will grow up to do the same. If you want to raise a happy, healthy child, teach them that you also have needs and that their bad behaviour can adversely affect you.

I advocate a gentle and loving parenting approach, but also firmly believe that children need healthy and realistic boundaries. This benefits both their emotional health as well as our own. When kids cross the boundaries we set for them, we must be able to communicate this without aggression or causing a fracture in our relationship.

The key to cooperation: Saying the right things

When our kids drive us to distraction, we often react and say things in the heat of the moment without thinking them through. These may include one or several of the following:

- *Blaming* them for something that may have happened, such as cereal being spilt, or mud being walked into the house.
- *Barking instructions* at them, such as, "Get out of my way!" or, "Clean that up immediately!"
- *Name calling*, perhaps labelling them as 'lazy', 'stupid' or 'selfish'.
- *Threatening* them with something like, "If you don't walk that dog, I'll give it away!" or, "You just wait until your dad hears about this!"
- *Comparing* them to their siblings or other children. We might say, "Why can't you do your homework like your sister does?"
- Using *sarcasm* to belittle or make fun of them. For instance, "So you haven't had a shower? Wondered what that smell was!" or " Is that your idea of neat handwriting? It is for a spider, maybe."
- *Predicting* their future with a comment such as, "You're so lazy... you'll never get a good job when you're older because you don't work hard enough."
- *Playing the victim*, where we put the focus on ourselves and how hard things are for us. We may say something like, " I've had such a hard day, and now you're just trying to make things worse for me. Can't you see I'm tired?" or, "You're making me old before my time! Is it any wonder I'm stressed all the time with you behaving like this?"

In times of conflict, comments such as these can be counterproductive. They may leave our kids feeling defensive, unloved, scared, defiant, guilty and worthless. This is no basis on which to try to gain cooperation or any kind of respect. Put yourself in their shoes - how would you feel?

But as you can hopefully now recognise, these are usually the reactions of a fraught parent, in a highly triggered and out-of-control state. Using the techniques I have previously described, we can instead approach such conflicts from a more peaceful and balanced place. Rather than resorting to any of the above tactics which are so damaging to children, causing resentment and complete disconnection, try using the following positive techniques:

Use 'I-phrases' instead of 'you-messages'

When you're annoyed about your child's behaviour, try to talk about *your feelings* rather than attacking their behaviour. Statements which contain 'you-messages' such as, "***You're*** late again! How many times have I got to tell ***you*** to be on time?" sound highly judgemental and confrontational.

Instead, stop blaming and shaming your child. Talk more about how their behaviour affects ***you*** and makes ***you feel***. When you do this, the way you sound to your child will change, and you'll start to include 'I-phrases' in what you say. So, if they come in late, rather than lecturing them on how selfish and unthoughtful they are, try saying, "***I get really anxious*** when you're not home on time."

Or if your child draws on the carpet, you could say, "It ***makes me very cross and upset*** to see our home ruined like that." This is better than screaming at them about the mess they have made. You may find it difficult to respond in this way at first. But remember that as long as you're not attacking them, a child is more likely to listen, cooperate and respect what you say.

Describe rather than berate

Rather than flooding your kids with a barrage of words about what ***they've done***, try to simply describe what ***you see*** and ***what the problem is***. For example, instead of lecturing them about always leaving their laptop on the floor, you could say, " Your laptop's on the floor. I'm concerned that it's going to get broken and I won't be able to afford to buy you a new one."

When using this technique, it's crucial to speak without judgement. This can be difficult and takes practice. It helps to get down to your child's level, make eye contact, describe what you see and how you are feeling using an 'I-phrase'. This may have little effect at first, and you might have to repeat yourself. But persevere, and your kids will soon understand this new form of communication.

So, when your child next leaves the bathroom floor covered in water, try saying, "The bathroom floor's wet, and I'm worried someone might slip and hurt themselves." There's no need to launch into a tirade about how you have to tell them the same thing every day and will they ever learn.

If they don't respond at first, get their attention again and repeat, "The floor needs drying, so nobody slips." Continue like this, using a calm and authoritative voice, until they get the message and do as you want them to do.

Remember that it's easier for kids to recognise and concentrate on a problem when it's clearly described to them. This also allows them to work out for themselves how to rectify the situation, teaching them problem-solving skills and independence.

Be informative, not corrective

Give clear information to your kids, without launching into a lecture, and you'll often get the response you want. For example, if they leave the lid off the toothpaste, try saying, "Toothpaste goes hard if the lid isn't put back on the tube." Avoid chastising them about how they always leave the lid off and how messy they are.

If their dirty washing is all over the floor, simply state that, "dirty clothes go in the laundry bin." No need to nag about the state of their room.

Once you've given the necessary information, wait for them to do what you want them to do. If they don't, ask them to stop what they're doing, look them in the eye and repeat the information. Stay calm and avoid getting into a debate over what you've said. Repeat this until they respond appropriately.

Speak like you're talking to a friend's child

If you're used to giving orders and instructions, it can be difficult to work out what tone you should now adopt when speaking to your kids. It can help to ask yourself how you would talk to a friend's child.

You'd never bark, " Go to bed!" But you might say, "Come on love, I think it's bedtime." By thinking about how you would address someone else's child, you tend to adopt a gentler and less confrontational tone.

Try being a little playful in your communication.

This can be infectious and lighten everyone's mood. Maybe you can find a way to speak in a silly voice, tell a crazy story or be a bit daft? It might surprise you to see how responsive your kids are when you make them laugh.

Kids hate lectures - so keep it short

We all know that when parents start rambling on and on, kids invariably switch off. So instead of giving them a sermon or a lengthy explanation, try getting your point across with a simple word.

Perhaps your child knows that they are meant to go for a shower every evening after dinner, but this is something they always try to avoid. Next time just say, "Shower, " and don't engage in further discussion on the matter. If it's their job to clean out the guinea pig, then a simple, "Guinea pig," will get your point across.

The power of a note

Sometimes a note can be a fun and engaging way to communicate with your kids. As it's non- verbal, it can catch their attention in a way that speaking doesn't. If your child is meant to feed the dog before doing their homework, try putting a note on their laptop that says, "Rover's hungry!"

If they're prone to turning on the Xbox the minute they get home, put a note on it saying, "Have I done my homework? Have I walked the dog? "

You perhaps don't want to leave notes too frequently, or they can start to lose their impact, but they can be a novel way to engage cooperation without the conflict.

Sometimes a very serious note may be appropriate. If your child has made you mad, then telling them how you feel in a letter could have the biggest impact. Obviously, what you say and how you say it always needs to be age appropriate. But for example, a note that said the following would certainly get the point across:

" *Sam,*

Leaving the house with the doors unlocked and the windows open put our home at risk. I'm really disappointed as I specifically asked you to lock them this morning.

Dad"

These are some simple techniques you can use to stop yourself shouting or saying things to your children which you might later regret. They won't work for all kids, and some of them may not sit comfortably with you, so just try the ones that feel right. But remember to be authentic. If you're attempting to sound sweet and gentle when you're actually fuming, your kids will know that you're not being genuine. This is unlikely to result in them responding positively to you.

Toddler specific techniques:

When a very young child is acting up, there are a few techniques that can work brilliantly to manage their behaviour:

Practise prevention

You know your child best, and you understand their triggers. Use this knowledge to steer off any tantrums and meltdowns. If you know that your little one is prone to emptying your kitchen cupboards and that this always ends in a tantrum when you try to stop them, put a lock on your cabinet doors. If they endlessly torment the dog, use stairgates to give your pet refuge and avoid the endless battles. Childproofing your home in this way can really help to reduce conflict with your kids.

Plan ahead

If your toddler is generally happier in the mornings, then do your supermarket shopping first thing. Don't leave it until the afternoon when they're tired and grumpy. Always pack a drink, snack and some toys to stave off boredom and avert meltdowns.

If you're planning something new, explain to your kids ahead of time where you're going and what will happen there. The more prepared they feel, the more likely they are to behave.

Distraction

I know this sounds so simple, but often the easiest techniques work best. When your child next starts niggling over something, try spotting a fascinating bug on the windowsill and get them to come and have a look. This interrupts their behaviour by catching their attention and distracting them from what was upsetting them.

If your toddler is insisting on knocking down their brother's bricks, then try saying, "Look what I can do!" and start driving cars around on the floor on the other side of the room. Their attention is likely to be quickly diverted, and they'll soon become absorbed in what you are doing.

Be silly

Sometimes using humour can be the best way to diffuse a situation. If your toddler won't put their socks on, try putting them on your ears! This will soon make them laugh, and your insistence that they belong on your ears will quickly make them want to correct you and show you that they do, in fact, belong on their feet.

This trick can also work wonders with a child who doesn't like putting their shoes on. Declare that you're going to put them on yourself and they'll instantly tell you not to be so silly. They'll insist that your feet are too big, that their shoes will only fit them, and will proceed to show you how...job done!

Use reverse psychology

You can easily interrupt a child's attempt at defiant behaviour by employing a bit of reverse psychology. The next time they don't want to eat their food, try telling them not to touch it while you go and do something else. Insist that *you* will eat it all up as soon as you return. The minute you turn your back, they'll gobble it up, finding your mock horror, when you come back to see it all gone, hilarious!

Chapter 7: What to do With Challenging Children

Let's be honest - sometimes, despite our very best efforts, some kids just have the propensity to go the extra mile in their challenging behaviour. Their ability to scream, shout and do the exact opposite to anything we may ask of them can be overwhelming. These occurrences can be severely minimised by employing the strategies I have described so far in this book, but they can still happen.

In attempting to be a peaceful parent, some people may think the only option is to give in, take a permissive approach, and allow their kids to 'win'. In my experience, this only stores up trouble for the future. It may solve the immediate problem, as the child will soon calm down when given what they want. But, in the longer term, it actually only serves to teach them that to get their own way, they need to misbehave. They learn that negative behaviour will ultimately lead to their parent capitulating and giving in to their demands. This is not a lesson we want to teach our kids, and it will do nothing to serve them in later life. So, what can we do? Here are some strategies which can help:

Expect resistance - things won't change overnight

If your kids are accustomed to you shouting to get them to behave, then you may find that at first, they don't respond positively to a fresh approach. Fighting you will have become their norm. Naturally, it will take time to turn things around. But it's worth the effort - just stick with it.

In Chapter 2, we discussed why punishment doesn't work, and the harm it can cause our kids and our relationships with them. But when they blatantly disobey us, we may feel like every fibre of our being screams out that the only solution is to punish them! We tell ourselves that without punishment, we risk losing control. We fear submitting to their will and becoming a permissive parent. What if we end up powerless in the face of our defiant children?

These fears are entirely justified. But it's crucial to understand that a child who misbehaves needs to *experience the consequences of their behaviour*, and not a punishment. Our goal is to get them to genuinely feel sorry for what they have done, and to concern themselves with how to put things right. We want them to have empathy for those they have hurt, and develop their own inner processes for dealing with the situation. This teaches them how to self-regulate and make the right decisions in the future.

When kids are punished, they only focus on what has been inflicted on them and how sorry they feel for themselves having to endure it. They become entirely self-centred with little regard or remorse for what they did in the first place, or how it may have affected others. This is the fundamental reason why punishment doesn't work when dealing with challenging behaviour.

Be authoritative, not authoritarian

When your kids are misbehaving, the most important thing is to keep control of yourself, as described in chapter 4. Recognise that you are highly likely to find this a triggering situation and take all the necessary steps to avoid getting wound up.

When your child is in meltdown, it's actually a frightening experience for them, and they need you to step up and take charge. But there is an important point to be made here. You need to manage the situation without becoming dominating or intimidating.

Avoid labels

Beware of labelling your kids. The words you speak over them will stay with them for life. Such is the power of a self-fulfilling prophecy. If we label kids as 'naughty', 'selfish' or 'stupid', then the chances are they will think of themselves in these terms and live up to these labels in the future. For example, if we endlessly call them 'lazy,' they may well internalise this and not push themselves as hard as they might otherwise have done.

Even if we don't speak our labels out loud, we need to be careful how we think about our kids. The beliefs we hold about them will affect how we interact with them, our expectations of them and what we believe they are capable of. Sometimes it only takes a look or a tone of voice for a child to understand clearly what their parents think of them.

Are you really listening carefully?

You may think you know what is causing your child to misbehave but do you really? Try to take a moment to get down to their level and ask them to explain why they are upset, even if the answer seems obvious to you.

Sometimes what they say is not what you expect. In some cases, the root cause may be something that can be quickly addressed. They may want to take their favourite teddy to the shops, or they might need a drink. Offering quick practical solutions may be enough to calm them, so you can get on with what you need them to do.

Always make sure that their basic needs have been met first; that they are not hungry, thirsty, tired, unwell or uncomfortable. Don't ignore these and always address them before trying to move forward with the situation.

Perhaps the problem is a little more complex. Maybe they feel anxious in crowded places and consequently don't want to go to the supermarket. Do they get car sick and, if so, are they worried about driving to your destination? Perhaps they feel bored or shy at your friend's house, which is why they want to stay at home.

By listening carefully to our kids, we sometimes discover that they have an underlying fear, worry or concern that we were unaware of. Taking steps to help them with this can go a long way to resolving any issues and lead to significant improvements in their behaviour.

What are their objections, and do they have a point?

If you insist that your child should wear a coat on a warm day, then perhaps it would be reasonable to concede that it's not in fact necessary. If they want their ears pierced, because they are the only one in their friendship group without them, then maybe this is something worth considering.

We don't always have to win the argument for the sake of it. Look at things objectively. If your child has a point, then there is nothing wrong with acknowledging that.

Name what they are feeling

Sometimes there may be nothing we can do to get our kids to behave. We've met all their basic needs. They're just screaming and shouting because they are, and they don't always understand what they are feeling or why.

When a child is in this state, it's important to tune into their emotional storm and name their feelings for them. This helps them to learn to communicate and articulate their emotions. It also gives them the reassurance that you understand how they are feeling, even if they don't.

Try saying something like, "I know you're cross because you want that toy, but we are shopping for bread and milk now. We can get your cars out when we get home." This tells them that you understand why they are upset and names their emotion. It also may help to soothe them as you've given them something else to focus on; a game they enjoy and which they can look forward to when they get home.

If your 10-year-old is sad because none of her friends are free for a playdate, then let her know that it's ok to feel disappointed and a bit lonely. Reassure her that she'll see them soon and suggest an activity that you could do together instead. Again, this helps her to understand what she is feeling, names her emotions and gives her something positive to focus on.

Are you communicating clearly?

Don't always assume that your requests have been understood. Make sure that your child understands what it is you want from them. Try making statements about what you want instead of vague, generalised comments: "Please sit down," is more specific and clearer than, "Dinner time."

Ensure that you're close to your child and have their full attention before giving an instruction. Calling from the next-door room or upstairs for them to brush their teeth may result in them not hearing you, or you being ignored.

Make sure your instructions are age-appropriate

If your child is younger, keep things simple and use words they understand. When talking to older children, be clear without being patronising.

If you give them too many instructions at once, they may find this overwhelming. Instead, give one instruction one at a time, waiting for them to complete each task before issuing a new one.

Explain the rules

Sometimes it may not be evident to your kids why a certain rule is in place or why you are asking them to do a particular thing. Make sure your reasons are clear and have always been well explained.

Avoid saying things that will seem unreasonable to them. For instance, telling them they need to do something "because you said so" is likely to backfire. This does nothing to help them understand why a task is necessary or must be completed.

If your child is refusing to share their toys, it would be better to say, " If you take a toy from your friend, it upsets them because they still want to play with it. You can have a turn in a minute." This teaches them empathy and the reason why they must share, even if they still don't particularly like the idea.

Be sure to keep your explanations simple and to the point. Too many words will quickly dilute your message, and you risk losing your child's attention.

Present your child with a clear and immediate choice

Often kids have meltdowns when they feel overwhelmed or that they have no control in a situation. This can frequently be resolved by offering two or three specific choices which are still related to the task that needs doing.

If you want your toddler to hold the buggy while you walk up the street without running off, try saying, " You have a choice. You can either walk and hold the buggy, or you can be strapped in."

Maybe your kids don't want to go to the shops, but leaving them at home isn't an option. Ask them if they would prefer to walk or go on their scooter. This can often make a shopping trip a bit more appealing.

If you tell your child to tidy their room, this may seem like an enormous job which they don't know how to tackle. Instead, try breaking it down into smaller tasks and asking, "Would you like to put your dolls in the box first or tidy away your shoes?" These both seem like easy manageable options, and when they've done one of them, praise them and then present the next choice. Before you know it, you'll have a tidy room without all the drama.

Perhaps you are going out for dinner and they're is refusing to wear what you want them to. This calls for some compromise, so allow them to choose between a couple of outfits which you know they like, but which are also acceptable to you.

When your kids need to do their homework, get them to choose which piece to complete first, rather than dictating what they will do and in which order.

By giving choices such as these, you can remain in charge while allowing them to feel like they have some control too.

Act quickly when you need to

If your child refuses the options you give them, then choose one for them, and ensure it is carried out. Next time, they'll be far more likely to cooperate and choose for themselves.

So, let's take the situation where you have given them the choice to either walk and hold the buggy, or be strapped in. But instead, they choose to ignore you and try to run off. It's important to catch them and immediately say, "I see you decided to get strapped in." Then quickly clip them into the buggy without further debate.

It's essential that the choices you offer are clear and that you make sure that one of them is carried out. If your child resists, don't start wavering or being indecisive. Don't add additional options or blur your boundaries by allowing them you start a debate with you. Instead, act quickly and assertively. This way they'll learn that you mean what you say and that the choices you present are the only ones available to them.

Give your child adequate warning and time to process

Give your kids notice that they will need to stop what they are doing soon because they need to do something else. They're more likely to respond positively to this than if you suddenly issue a command without warning.

Imagine your child is busy watching TV. You announce, "In ten minutes when that programme has finished, I want you to come and do your reading." This is likely to get a better reaction than suddenly saying, "Turn that off and do your reading."

Equally, once you have given an instruction, wait a few seconds without saying anything, to give them a chance to process and respond to what you have said. Sometimes kids don't act as fast as we would like. We get cross almost immediately when actually all they need is a moment to get into gear.

This approach also teaches children to respond to instructions the first time they hear them. Parents can often get into the habit of repeating themselves multiple times. This teaches their kids that they can afford to ignore them at first, and only need to respond after several repetitions, once their parent is annoyed.

Give them a way to help

When a child has done something wrong, they may feel out of their depth and unsure what to do next. The situation can often be resolved by giving them an immediate way to help.

If they have just spilt water all over the floor, offer them a cloth and say, "You could use this to clean it up." This gives them a quick solution to the problem and may prevent the need for any further conflict.

Consequences

In chapter 2, we discussed punishments and why they don't work. But there should always be consequences for unacceptable behaviour. Let's take a moment to discuss these in more detail, and look at the best way to use consequences effectively.

Let kids experience the direct consequences of their behaviour

This can be tough, but it's important to allow kids to experience the repercussions of their own decisions.

If your toddler bites another child at playgroup, remove them immediately and take them home. But it's essential to explain that you are going home because they hurt another child and children don't want to play with kids who hurt them.

If your child takes food to their room and drops crumbs everywhere, ensure that they clean up the mess.

If they refuse to tidy their room, then don't allow them to go on a playdate that evening. Explain that they need to use the time to finish tidying up instead.

If they don't put their football kit in the wash, leave it where they drop it. They may have to wear it dirty for their next training session, but I guarantee that they'll remember to put it in the laundry basket next time!

If they do a poor job of their homework project, let them take it to school incomplete. Don't step in and patch it up to stop them getting into trouble.

In this way, kids soon learn what they need to do to avoid negative consequences. I know it's hard not to jump in and do things for them. I struggle with this too. But view it as teaching them a life skill. How will they ever learn to fend for themselves if we continually come to their rescue?

Consequences to avoid

1: Negative attention

Giving plenty of praise and positive attention is an excellent reward for good behaviour and teaches your child that this is the right way to behave. But the opposite is not true for poor behaviour.

If you react to unwanted behaviour by shouting and giving negative attention, it will only get worse over time. A child would rather have **any** attention from you, either good or bad, than none at all. So, keeping your cool in the face unacceptable behaviour is by far the best thing to do. Instead, stay calm, explain what is wrong, how you feel about it and what needs to happen next to put things right.

2: Positive consequences

It's important that kids don't get what they want by misbehaving. If your child won't put their own shoes on, and insists that you do it for them when they are perfectly able to do it themselves, don't give in.

If your 4-year-old refuses to walk, don't carry them. If they're screaming for a toy in a shop, don't buy it for them just to get them to be quiet.

By giving into kids' demands in this way, we teach them that there are positive consequences for poor behaviour, and that they'll get what they want when they behave badly.

If you have asked them to wash up and they either don't do it or do a poor job, resist the urge to do it for them. You may need to supervise and guide them to ensure it's done properly, but it's important that they complete any tasks given.

If we ask for something to be done, as long as the request is both reasonable and age-appropriate in the first place, we must see it through.

3: Disproportionate and inconsistent consequences

No matter how much our kids make us see red, it's important not to overreact when it comes to consequences. They should be proportionate and, if possible, a natural result of their misbehaviour. It's also vital to be consistent.

If you don't allow food upstairs today, but tomorrow you say it's ok, then you'll give your kids very confusing and mixed messages.

Imagine that your child is rude to their friend and as a result you ask them to sit in their room for half an hour and write a letter of apology. A similar situation occurs a month later, and this time, you tell them that they're grounded for a month with all privileges removed.

On another occasion, you and your child are having a chat over dinner. The mood is relatively light-hearted. They get a bit cheeky, so you tell them not to be rude and leave it at that. A few days later, after a particularly taxing day, they speak to you in the same tone as they did before. This time, you're in a terrible mood, shout at them for being disrespectful, confiscate their laptop for a week, and tell them that they can no longer go to their friend's birthday party at the weekend.

Inconsistencies and overreactions such as these can lead to our kids resenting us, believing that we are unpredictable and unfair. A massive consequence for a relatively small misdemeanour is going to leave them feeling demoralised. Over time they may even give up trying to behave at all.

Show the child how to make amends

When kids have done something wrong, they can often carry on misbehaving if they can't see a way to put things right. So, it helps to show them how they can make amends. It can be surprising how often this can lead to them doing the right thing, even if they take a little while to do so.

If your child didn't bother walking the dog this morning, you could say, "The dog needs a longer walk this afternoon as he didn't go out earlier."

If they've been rude to you, you could, once you have dealt with their behaviour, say, "I'd love a cup of tea." This gives them a way to clear the air so you can both move on.

Negotiation

But how do you handle persistently unacceptable behaviour? What do you do if you feel you've tried everything, and you still can't get your child to cooperate? A situation such as this may require a different approach, one where you work together with them to find a solution.

If your child is consistently defiant, it's essential to work out why. As a first step, talk the issue through with them to understand how they feel about it. Together, try to work out what is driving them to misbehave and what they need from the situation. It's crucial to stay calm and listen. Getting angry, upset or arguing will only make things worse. *Let this be their chance to speak.*

Second, *they need to hear you out too*. Explain that you listened to them without interrupting, and now it's only fair that they do the same for you. Describe how *you* feel about the situation and what your needs are. Again, try to stay calm and avoid getting upset.

Next, *write down all the possible solutions* you can *both* think of, without evaluating them yet. At this point, it will be apparent that some ideas are immediately not acceptable to you, but don't comment. Just write them all down - all your suggestions and all those presented by your child.

Finally, *work through your list together*, crossing out any ideas that either of you don't like. Try to find ones that you can agree on, even if this requires a little compromise. Decide together how to proceed and *put your plan into action*.

Negotiating in this way can be very effective, but it's not easy, particularly for an intuitively strict parent. We have to let go of the idea that as the parent, we are always right, know all the answers and that our child's behaviour is merely a problem that we need to fix. We have to stop worrying about losing power over them by giving up control.

It takes a significant shift in mindset to believe that together, we can reach a mutually acceptable resolution. But if we take time to share our feelings with our child, and acknowledge theirs, then this can be achieved. In adopting this approach, we're teaching our kids that they neither have to dominate or be dominated by us. They also learn the skills necessary to deal with conflict both at home and in the wider world.

Time out and how to use it effectively

Sometimes kids, just like us, need 'time out' from a highly stressful or difficult situation. When they have tantrums or lose their cool, they can become overwhelmed emotionally and need a little time to calm down before they can deal with the situation they're in. I, therefore, believe in using time out as a way to press pause; to give them a chance to regroup before needing to continue. It shouldn't be seen as a punishment for bad behaviour, but a tool to help them achieve what they have been asked to do.

It's also a way for them to recognise when they've overstepped a behaviour boundary that has been put in place for them. Older children can use time out as an opportunity to reflect on their choices and what would be appropriate for them to do next.

It's well documented that the most effective form of parenting is both warm and firm, in which kids are not given attention when they misbehave. Time out can be a fantastic tool for diffusing a problematic situation, giving both you and your child the space you need to calm down. But we should implement some basic steps for time out to work effectively:

Advanced warning

It's a good idea to explain to your kids ahead of time what 'time out' means and why you use it. Again, don't describe this as a punishment which you'll use if they misbehave. Instead, explain that sometimes people get very cross and frustrated and need a chance to calm down. Make clear that this is what causes kids to have tantrums and so by putting them in time out, you're helping them by giving them a chance to cool off.

Make sure that they understand which behaviours will result in them being put in time out, e.g. screaming, hitting, kicking, biting, throwing toys, spitting, etc. This will help them to know what to expect and when.

A time out spot

Some people find it helpful to have a place in their home that they use for time out; perhaps a step or a chair in a quiet part of the house. This should be away from the hustle and bustle of the main activities of the home. But you still need to be able to see your child to make sure they comply and don't hurt themselves.

Don't name your time out spot with a derogatory term such as 'the naughty chair' or anything similar. This is far more likely to make your kids view time out as a punishment rather than a tool to help them to calm their emotions.

Act quickly

As soon as your kids misbehave in a way that warrants time out, you must act quickly, calmly and decisively. Don't give any second chances. Avoid saying something like, "If you hit me again, you'll go into time out," and don't enter into discussion with them over their behaviour. Always state the reason for time out in a specific, short and unemotional way;" No biting… time out." This helps them to link their behaviour to the consequence.

How long should time out be?

Most experts agree that a reasonable length of time for time out is one minute per year of the child's age. It can be helpful to use a timer which they can see, so they know that the time is always fair and consistent.

What if my child won't stay in time out?

In this situation, it's vital to say calm, focused and consistent. Return your child to the time out spot, explain that they have to stay there until their time is complete and restart the timer. Stay nearby if necessary, to stop them from running off but do not engage with them. If they move away, return them and start again. This may be time consuming at first, but your child must learn that the boundaries you have put in place will not be moved.

Some experts recommend not starting the allocated time until your child has calmed down and is completely quiet. This may work for some kids, but for others, this will be too much to ask, particularly if they are young. Instead, make sure your child is quiet for 5 seconds before ending time out. This teaches them to associate the end of time out with calm, peaceful behaviour, and it sends the message that screaming during time out doesn't work.

Provide no attention or rewarding stimuli

While in time out, do not engage with your child. Also, do not let them hear you discussing them with others. By withdrawing your attention, (which they want more than anything,) they learn that misbehaving does not bring positive rewards.

While in time out, they should not be able to watch TV, play with toys, or watch their siblings play.

End with a positive word or hug

At the end of time out, when your child has settled, it's important to praise them for calming down. Sometimes it may only be appropriate to do this with words by saying something like, "Well done, I know you were angry. But you've managed to calm down." If you think they might be receptive, a hug could reassure them that everything is ok, that you still love them and that they can now safely move on.

If they are calm, but still a bit cross and don't want a hug, that's fine. Don't force it. Respect how they are feeling and go back to your day. They'll hug you when they are ready.

Don't insist that your child apologise at the end of a time out session. If they have managed to regain control of their emotions and calm down, then that is enough. Sometimes they will say sorry if they genuinely feel like it. But insisting on an empty apology if your child doesn't mean it, is pointless. If anything, this can cause matters to escalate again, resulting in further conflict.

Return to the task and turn your attention back on

It's essential that once your child has finished time out, that they complete any task they were asked to do before it began. Don't allow them to think time out can be a way for them to get out of doing these.

Turn your full attention back on and do your best to catch them 'being good' as soon as you can. When they show the slightest positive behaviour, it's important to notice and comment on it specifically. Don't be vague in your praise. If they start to put away the toys say, " Well done, that's great tidying up." This reassures them that they can behave well again and that your relationship is sound.

Chapter 8: The Power of Praise

E ven if you've been stuck in a negative rut with your kids, it's so important to notice when they are doing things right and praise them for it. But be careful how you do this, or they might reject your praise, believing it to be insincere, or manipulative. Worse still, kids can often be quick to dismiss any praise we give, considering it to be unfounded, and instead end up criticising themselves. Try using 'descriptive praise' instead. This has two parts to it:

1. First, you need to describe, with appreciation, what you see or feel. So, if your child shows you their latest picture, don't just say, "That's lovely." Instead, take time to describe what you see: " I love the colours you've used to do the sunset. They're gorgeous."

2. If your child can accept your praise, they are more likely to internalise it and actually then praise themselves. In the above example, instead of wondering if you really like their picture, they're more likely to accept that you do genuinely like it. After all, you took the time to study it, and describe it in such detail. They may then admit that they are, in fact, pretty good at art.

Using praise in this way can help kids become more aware and accepting of their own strengths. But it takes effort. It's much easier to say, "That's great!" than to actively spend time analysing and describing what they have done. The reason this works is that it's another way of giving your kids your attention, so they feel noticed, valued and appreciated.

Descriptive praise can be made more powerful by adding words that highlight your child's praiseworthy behaviour. Then your praise is no longer just about the thing they have done. It's also about them as a person. An example may be, "I love the colours you used in your picture. You're so **creative**." Or," You took such wonderful care of your friend today. You were really **thoughtful**." This is most effective if you can find a word to tell them something about themselves that they may not have known or considered before.

If you use this approach regularly, your child will learn so much about their strengths. They can then store this information away in their emotional piggy bank and use it to build a positive self-image.

Help them see themselves differently

This can be difficult as a parent, but we need to admit if we have given our kids negative labels in the past. Perhaps we have called them lazy, messy or selfish? In Chapter 6 we talked about how damaging these comments can be.

When kids hold these destructive self-beliefs, it's crucial to help them see themselves in a new light. If they believe that they are lazy, we could comment on how hard they worked on tidying their room. If they see themselves as stupid, describing how well they did a piece of difficult homework could really boost their confidence.

It can help to put kids in *practical situations* which challenge their perceptions about themselves. If they think we don't trust them, then we need to prove that this isn't true. Perhaps give them some money to put in the school raffle. If they believe they are clumsy, then handing them something fragile to carry shows we have confidence in their ability not to break it.

Each time we put them in situations which challenge their misconceptions about themselves, we break the power of any labels spoken over them, and their self-esteem begins to grow.

Let them hear you singing their praises

Nothing fills a child with pride more than hearing their parents speaking positively about them to others. So if our kids have negative beliefs about themselves, we can use conversations with other people to break these ideas down.

If they think they're forgetful, we can let them hear us telling someone about how brilliantly they memorised their lines for the school play. If they class themselves as cowardly, we can ensure they overhear us chatting to a friend about how brave they were at their new karate lesson.

Final word: Embracing the role of the peaceful parent

The road to becoming a peaceful parent is a long and winding one. It's not something that will happen overnight, especially if you have been treading a different path for a long while. Remember that old habits die hard, and it will take time, dedication and persistence to turn things around.

Each child is different, and what works for one may not necessarily work for another. Think of the techniques I have shared with you here as tools to help you on your way. Experiment with them to find what suits you and your family best. Remember that no parent is perfect; we all get it wrong sometimes. Don't beat yourself up when this happens. Instead, learn from your mistakes and carry on striving to do better. It's all about making progress; building on our successes little by little. After all, there is no such thing as perfection.

The most essential ingredient in all of this is love. Make sure that your kids feel your unconditional love for them each and every day, regardless of whether they are behaving like angels or little terrors. Children who know they are loved unconditionally are more likely to grow up into emotionally healthy adults, capable of facing all of life's hurdles.

I hope that the techniques in this book have shown you how to develop positive relationships with your children, based on good communication, mutual understanding and respect. May your home become a harmonious place, full of love and laughter. Remember that peaceful parenting may have its challenges, but the rewards are priceless.

Bibliography

Adams, Cathy. *Living What You Want Your Kids To Learn*. Be U, an imprint of Wyatt-MacKenzie, 2014.

"How to Give Kids Effective Instructions" *Child Mind institute*. https://child-mind.org/article/how-to-give-kids-effective-instructions/

"How to Make Time Out Work" Child Mind Institute https://child-mind.org/article/how-to-make-time-outs-work/

"Managing Problem Behaviour at Home" *Child Mind Institute* https://child-mind.org/article/managing-problem-behavior-at-home/

Clark, Alicia."5 Tips for Disciplining a Difficult Child" https://aliciaclarkp-syd.com/how-to-discipline-a-difficult-child/

Clarke-Fields, Hunter. *Raising Good Humans - A Mindful Guide to Breaking the Cycle of Reactive Parenting and Raising Kind, Confident Kids.* New Harbinger Publications, Inc, 2019

Cohen, Lawrence J. *Playful Parenting*. New York: Ballantine Books, 2001

Editors of Child Magazine."How to Put An End to Difficult Behavior." *Parents Blog* https://www.parents.com/toddlers-preschoolers/discipline/tips/how-to-put-an-end-to-difficult-behavior/

Faber, Adele & Mazlish, Elaine. *How to Talk so Kids Will Listen & Listen so Kids Will Talk.* Piccadilly Press, London,1982

Gershoff, Elizabeth T et al. 2010. "Parent Discipline Practices in an International Sample: Associations with Child Behaviors and Moderation by Perceived Normativeness." *Child Development* 2010: 81(2): 487–502.

Hall, Astrid. " Parents Feel Stressed Six Times a Day Because of Their Children, Study Claims." *Independent Blog* 2018
   https://www.independent.co.uk/life-style/health-and-families/parents-stress-children-six-times-a-day-study-results-anxiety-mum-dad-a8574086.html

"Understanding the Stress Response." *Harvard health Publishing*, Harvard Medical School, 2018, https://www.health.harvard.edu/staying-healthy/understanding-the-stress-response

Ireland, Tom. "What Does Mindfulness Meditation Do to Your Brain?" *Scientific American Blog.* June 2014 https://blogs.scientificamerican.com/guest-blog/what-does-mindfulness-meditation-do-to-your-brain

McCraith, Sheila. *Yell Less Love More.* Boston: Fair Winds Press, 2014.

Naumburg, Carla. *How to Stop Losing Your Sh*t With Your Kids. Effective Strategies for Stressed Out Parents.* Yellow Kite. An imprint of Hodder & Stoughton, 2019.

Neff, Kristin. *Self-Compassion.* New York: William Morrow, an imprint of HarperCollins Publishers,2011.

Miller, Caroline. "How to Handle Tantrums and Meltdowns." *Child Mind Institute* https://childmind.org/article/how-to-handle-tantrums-and-meltdowns/

"Need to Know Guides - Positive Parenting" NSPCC 2019 https://learning.nspcc.org.uk/media/1195/positive-parenting.pdf

Pfaff, Leslie Garisto."9 Secrets to Toddler Discipline" *Parents blog* https://www.parents.com/toddlers-preschoolers/discipline/tips/secrets-to-toddler-discipline/?

Seltzer, Leon F. "You Only Get More of What You Resist—Why?" *Psychology Today*. 15 June 2016 https://www.psychologytoday.com/us/blog/evolution-the-self/201606/you only-get-more-what-you-resist-why

.

Find Out More

If you'd be interested in finding out find out more about me, or need further resources to help you on your parenting journey, then please visit my website at:

www.as-they-grow.com.

I'd just like to thank you so much for reading this book. I hope you enjoyed it and found it helpful!

If you did, please could you spare a moment to leave me a book review on Amazon?

You can do this by clicking on the *'Write a Customer Review'* button on the Amazon page where you bought this book.

I'd really appreciate it, and this would help boost the book's ranking on Amazon and allow me to reach more people.

Thanks so much for your time,

Nadine x

Also by Nadine Williamson

Do you want to know how to help your child grow into a capable, confident and self-reliant adult?

We all want the very best for our kids. But in the midst of our busy lives, we can easily overlook the need to teach some of the fundamental skills of life. This easy-to-follow booklet highlights 27 essential life skills that all children need to thrive as independent and resourceful people.

27 Essential Life Skills to Help Your Child Thrive
Here's a summary of what you'll learn:

· What life skills are and why it's so crucial to our kids' success to be taught them at a young age.

· Practical strategies for teaching a range of cognitive life skills such as the ability to focus, empathise, develop a sense of curiosity and a willingness to learn.

· How to instil excellent communication skills, improve memory, develop the ability to solve problems and think critically.

· Techniques for instilling self-discipline, organisational skills and a sense of responsibility.

· How to help your kids cope with failure, develop their self-esteem and learn to stand up for themselves.

· Dozens of tips for teaching your kids practical life skills so they can function competently and independently in the years ahead.

· From how to do the laundry, develop good timekeeping, or manage their money; you'll find plenty of advice on how to get them involved in the mechanics of everyday life to learn those essential skills.

There's something here for every parent: whether you have toddlers or teens, dip in and be inspired to teach a new skill today.

Printed in Great Britain
by Amazon

80785476R10051